Essential SLOW COOKER Recipes

 Carol Heding Munson

MAIN STREET

Art Director: Megan Kirby
Photostyling: Theresa Gwynn
Photographer: Evan Bracken, Light Reflections
Food Prep and Styling: David Rowland and Robert Wysong,
Executive Sous Chefs, Grove Park Inn Resort and Spa
Editor: Dawn Cusick

1 3 5 7 9 10 8 6 4 2

Published by Sterling Publishing Co., Inc.
387 Park Avenue South, New York, NY 10016

Distributed in Canada by Sterling Publishing
Canadian Manda Group, One Atlantic Avenue, Suite 105
Toronto, Ontario, Canada M6K 3E7

Distributed in Australia by Capricorn Link (Australia) Pty Ltd.
P.O. Box 704, Windsor, NSW 2756, Australia

Printed in China

Sterling ISBN 1-4027-0638-3

TABLE OF CONTENTS

INTRODUCTION

My situation is hardly unique: At the end of an 8- or 9-hour business day when I'm bushed and the family's hungry, there's nothing more rewarding than the aroma of a home-cooked meal. Even as I write this, I can hear the clamors: "What's for dinner? When do we eat?" Regardless of how busy our families are, though, everyone wants a nice meal. Fast-food takeout or something made in the microwave is fine every once in a while, but what everyone really wants is to sit down to a delicious, home-cooked meal. This book will show you the way to an incredible variety of wonderful, home-cooked meals that will fit into your busy schedule. The recipes for each presented here have all been designed to let you have a home-cooked meal waiting for you when you get home or shortly thereafter. And, after you've finished enjoying one of these great recipes, you'll enjoy the second benefit to one-pot cooking: easy clean up.

I have enjoyed cooking with a crockery pot, or slow cooker, for many years. Early in the day, when I feel fresh, I can toss a few ingredients into the slow cooker, then let it do its thing: simmer up a robust stew, or a light soup, or a flavorful pasta sauce. In the evening, when I'm ready to eat, dinner's done. As my success with this style of cooking grew, I wanted to share my best experiences with other cooking enthusiasts. What followed is this book, which is packed with quick-fix entrees, side dishes, and desserts.

These recipes are good for you—meaning low in fat and low in sodium. What's more, each has an incredible marriage of flavors that comes only from lengthy cooking. From the international favorites to the home-style dishes, every recipe that appears here had to pass muster not only with adults who enjoy gourmet foods, but also with my teenagers—independent critics with sharp taste buds and uninhibited opinions. Only the tastiest recipes survived. You should feel free to experiment with your own variations—who knows, you may even create enough favorite new combinations to fill your own cookbook. And along the way you'll experience another reward of slow cooking: the sensory pleasure of coming home to mouthwatering aromas.

Carol Heding Munson

BASICS
❧ ABOUT CROCKERY POTS ☙

The crockery pot is very energy efficient. When set to LOW, it actually draws less electricity than a 100-watt light bulb. The crockery pot, therefore, is economical to use and won't overheat the kitchen, even when simmering a roast for 10 to 12 hours. It also fits nicely on any countertop and stores handily in pantries as well.

Here are more reasons to take it slow: Gentle all-day simmering tenderizes lean meats and sturdy vegetables (carrots, rutabagas, potatoes, winter squash) for high-flavor, low-fat meals. And low cooking temperatures—200°F (93°C) when set on LOW; 300°F (150°C) on HIGH—mean that timing is flexible. A half-hour more or less won't spoil your meal.

Still more advantages: Most crockery pot recipes can be put together in 15 to 30 minutes. The cook need only measure and chop the ingredients, toss everything into the pot, and turn it on. (Some recipes also suggest sautéing meat, onions, or other ingredients before cooking for added flavor.) Several hours later, depending on the heat setting selected and the fullness of the pot, dinner's done. Could meal preparation get any easier or quicker? Well, perhaps, two meals for the work of one. Now, we're cooking! Depending on the size of the pot, crockery pots can handle food for a small crowd, so you can easily double small recipes or select ones that make 8 or 10 servings.

❧ COOKER STYLES ☙

Crockery pots come in two basic shapes—round and rectangular—and in medium and large sizes that range from 3 to 6 quarts. Less common are mini 1- and 2-quart crockery pots. Most of the minis, which may be battery operated, are electric and are designed to work on standard household current. Cords are short, so units must be placed near outlets.

At the core of most round crockery pots is a heavy ceramic bowl, which may or may not be removable. The bowl is surrounded by a metal sheaf that encases electric heating coils. Rectangular crockery pots have a removable nonstick metal bowl (really more like a high-sided pan) that sits on a multi-purpose base, which encloses a heating element with a temperature selection dial. Depending on the model and price, both types can be bought with either snug-fitting glass or lightweight plastic lids. The plastic lids stay somewhat cooler to the touch, but may turn opaque if you use your cooker a lot.

Buying a new crockery pot? Check out seasonal sales at major chain stores for price discounts up to 50%. Be sure to get one with a removable bowl even if it costs a bit more. It's worth the few extra dollars. Why? You can submerge the bowl in water for easy washing. And you can stash it in the refrigerator if you've prepared ingredients beforehand. When you're ready to cook, simply return the bowl to the unit and turn the switch on. Both ceramic and metal bowls are oven-safe, although ceramic ones aren't broiler-safe and metal ones can't go in a microwave. Ceramic bowls aren't for stove-top use, either; any sautéing before cooking must be done in a skillet—a minor inconvenience.

The beauty of a crockery pot is its plug-and-cook feature: toss everything in the pot, switch it on, and let the pot do its cooking thing. But can it really go the distance unattended? Yes, for the most part. Experience indicates that some foods, such as pot roasts that cook for 10 hours, will occasionally stick in cookers that have bottom-only heating elements. An infrequent stir—once every two hours or so—takes care of the problem.

For even cooking, dishes that require very little liquid can benefit from a stir as well. About halfway through cooking, stir to reverse the ingredients on the top and those on the bottom. Enjoy experimenting with your crockery pot; recipes react differently to each one, depending on things like bowl size, type of crockery pot, heat setting, and food density.

When it comes to cooking times, expect differences. All crockery pots are not necessarily equal. The accuracy of a crockery pot's thermostat and the location of heating elements (surrounding a ceramic bowl or below a metal one) can speed or slow cooking by a couple of hours. Is one better than another? It's difficult to say, since other factors also come into play: voltage fluctuations, how cold food is at the start of cooking, how often the lid is picked up, how full the crockery pot is, and the density of ingredients. No matter which crockery pot you select—or already have—plan on adjusting recipe times and sometimes increasing or decreasing the heat. Play around with your cooker and you'll get to know its character.

✺ COOKING BASICS BY FOOD GROUP ✺

Is your appetite up for some seriously delicious slow cooking? The following guidelines will help smooth the transition from stove top to crockery pot cooking.

Meats and Poultry

- Buy roasts in sizes and shapes that fit your cooker. Otherwise, you'll have to hunt up a meat cleaver and cut them to fit.
- Use lean cuts of meat and poultry for low-fat meals. Before cooking, trim away all visible fat and remove poultry skin.

- Brown ground beef, lamb, chicken, and turkey in a skillet over medium-high heat to give chilies, pasta sauces, and other dishes rich flavor and appealing dark color. To brown the low-fat way, use a nonstick skillet and mist it with a nonstick spray. After the meat is browned, transfer it to the slow cooker, using a slotted spoon so excess fat remains in the skillet.
- Cook cubed beef, chicken, pork, and turkey on LOW for up to 10 hours, but check them after 7 hours. They may be done. For added flavor, brown the cubes before putting them in the crockery pot.
- Add visual appeal and rich braised flavor by browning roasts before cooking them in the crockery pot.

7

Vegetables

- Place dense root vegetables, such as carrots, turnips, celery root, potatoes, onions, and rutabagas, on the pot bottom, and keep them submerged in the liquid for uniform cooking. Top vegetables with meat (though it's hard to believe, meat cooks faster than the root crops); pour liquids in last.
- Chop vegetables into consistent sizes for even cooking. Bite-size is always good, and ½"–2" sticks are attractive for Asian-style dishes.
- Stir in frozen peas, cut green beans, and mixed vegetables during the last 15 to 30 minutes of cooking if quantities are small (about ½ cup).
- Add tender vegetables (such as peas and snow peas); strongly flavored vegetables (such as broccoli, brussels sprouts, and cauliflower); and greens (such as kale, spinach, and escarole) during the last 15 to 60 minutes of cooking. Adding large quantities of last-minute goodies will temporarily lower the temperature of the cooking food. Timing depends on how much you're putting in.
- Brown onions and other vegetables to add caramelized color and flavor to dishes. Use the same low-fat techniques described for browning meats and poultry.

Pasta, Rice, and Other Grains

- Use long-grain rices. In slow cooking, they give the fluffiest results.
- Stir in raw rice and barley during the last 1 to 1½ hours of cooking. All-day cooking would result in gummy, almost gelatinous and gloppy grains. Use an extra ¼ cup water for every ¼ cup of raw grain. Alternate solution: Cook grains by conventional stove-top and microwave methods; then stir them in during the last 15 minutes. Brown and wild rice buffs take note: The cooking time for brown rice is approximately twice that of white rice. Wild rice takes even longer than brown.
- Add pasta to soups during the last 5 to 10 minutes of cooking. For other dishes, cook pasta on the stove top, then drain it, and top or toss it with the crockery pot ingredients right before serving. Whichever way it's cooked, pasta is best when done al dente.

Dried Beans

- Cooking time varies with bean types and the ingredients cooked with them. Baby limas, great northern beans, and small white beans take less cooking than garbanzos (chick-peas) and kidney beans. Dried beans will roughly double their volume when cooked.
- Boil garbanzo and red kidney beans with three times their volume of water in a large pot on the stove top for 10 minutes. Drain the beans in a colander and discard the water. Add the beans to other ingredients in the crockery pot.
- Soften beans completely before combining them with sweeteners (including brown sugar, honey, maple syrup, and molasses) or acid foods (such as vinegar or tomatoes), which actually harden legumes during cooking. Here's an easy way to do it:

8

Boil beans for 10 minutes, then reduce the heat, cover the pot, and allow the beans to simmer until they're tender, about 1½ hours. Discard the water. Add to ingredients in the crockery pot.

Cheese, Milk, and Other Dairy Products
- Stir cheese, sour cream, yogurt, and cream into main dishes, soups, and stews right before serving. Then cook just long enough to melt the cheese and heat all the ingredients. If cooked for hours, dairy foods tend to separate and look curdled.
- Opt for processed cheeses, which can tolerate heat fairly well, if you must cook cheese for a long period.
- Add milk just before serving, except in dessert recipes created to cook in two to three hours. Milk curdles with lengthy cooking.
- Try canned evaporated skim milk for the longest curdle-free cooking. In many dishes, it makes an excellent low-fat alternative to cream.

Fish

- Stir in shellfish—minced clams, shrimp, scallops—during the last 15 to 60 minutes of cooking, depending on quantity. Shellfish toughens if cooked for long periods.
- Mix in bite-size chunks of sturdy fish such as salmon and shark during the last 30 to 60 minutes of cooking. Cook until done. (To check for doneness, test the fish with a fork. Fully cooked fish should flake easily.)
- Don't use delicate fish such as flounder. It won't hold up during lengthy cooking.

❧ SECRETS TO SUCCESS ☙

Okay, now you've had the basic course in slow cooking. What follows are eight other helpful hints for sure-fire crockery pot success.
- Adjust seasonings at the end of cooking. Some spices, such as black pepper, intensify with lengthy cooking. Others, such as basil and garlic, become diluted and less pungent. Rule of thumb, er…spice: Include whole spices at the beginning of cooking; stir in ground spices and tender herbs at the end. Before serving, taste your creation, and spice it up as desired.
- Garnish dishes for visual pizzazz. Colors fade with lengthy cooking, and a simple garnish can really brighten things up. Here's a handful of off-the-shelf suggestions:

  Chopped, seeded tomatoes   *Crumbled bacon*
  Dollop of sour cream, yogurt, or cottage cheese   *Grated cheese*
  Ground nutmeg or ground paprika   *Slivered, sliced, or ground nuts*
  Wedges or slices of lemon, lime, or orange.   *Toasted croutons*
  Sprigs of parsley, rosemary, thyme or other herbs   *Fresh ground black or white pepper*

- Use small quantities of liquids when cooking soups. Before serving, thin the soup to an appropriate consistency with water, broth, tomato juice, or milk. Cover and heat on HIGH until hot, 15 to 60 minutes.
- Jump-start cooking by setting the crockery pot on HIGH for the first hour.
- Resist peeking. Every time you lift the lid, cooking time is extended, because crockery pots aren't designed to crank up the heat when some escapes. These are slow, steady gizmos, from the start of

cooking to the finish. Remove the lid only during the last half of cooking and do so only to stir food or check doneness.
- Prepare ingredients ahead, if you want, to make best use of your available time. But be certain to follow the food-safety suggestions in "Safety at Slow Speeds."
- Fill crockery pots half to three-quarters full, advise manufacturers. Refer to the instructions accompanying your crockery pot for more information.
- Increase cooking times as necessary if you live at a high altitude.

❧ SAFETY AT SLOW SPEEDS ❧

Food-safety experts assure us that cooking at low temperatures, 200°F (93°C) for LOW and 300°F (150°C) for HIGH, is completely safe if you follow these simple, common-sense guidelines:
- Keep all perishable ingredients in the refrigerator until you're ready to start cooking.
- Package raw meats and vegetables separately if you're preparing them ahead. You can place either meat or vegetables in the crockery pot bowl, cover, and refrigerate it, but don't mix the two until you're ready to cook.
- Never partially cook meat or poultry and finish cooking it later. If you'll be sautéing or browning foods, do so right before adding them to the crockery pot and turning it on.
- Check the doneness of roasts with a quick-read thermometer. In a matter of seconds, this handy little gadget will give you a read-out on the meat's internal temperature. The thermometers are available in most cook shops and many large supermarkets.
- Avoid using large quantities of completely frozen foods in your crockery pot. It's fine to add up to a cup of frozen peas to a potful of hot soup, but starting a recipe with a pound of frozen beef cubes or a frozen turkey breast is a no-no. A crockery pot isn't designed to defrost foods; using it for that purpose can result in gastrointestinal woes. Avoid the risk: Always thaw foods in the refrigerator or microwave; then slow cook them.
- Refrigerate leftovers quickly—certainly within two hours. If food has been on the table longer than that, don't take a chance. Throw it out. Bacteria thrive at room temperatures.
- Never reheat foods in a crockery pot. For safety's sake, previously cooked foods should come to a boil quickly. Reheat on the stove top or in a microwave.

❧ KITCHEN WISDOM ❧

Some of the following tips may seem obvious, and others may appear in the manufacturer's instruction booklet, but all bear repeating:
- Avoid sudden temperature changes. Really cold food or water can crack a hot ceramic bowl.
- Always use your crockery pot with the lid on. It's the only way slow cooking works!
- Don't immerse the heating elements in water.
- Turn off or unplug your crockery pot when you are done using it. (Some models have no on/off switch.)

❧ THICKENING SAUCES AND GRAVIES ❧

Is your sauce or gravy thin and watery? That's common with many dishes, including slow-cooked ones. It's up to the cook to make them thick, rich, and smooth. Fortunately, thickening is easy once you know the techniques and the proper proportions of starchy thickener to liquid. For slow-cooked foods, any of the common thickeners work just fine. Choose arrowroot, cornstarch, flour, or tapioca. Here are the specifics on what to do.

Arrowroot and Cornstarch: At the end of cooking, turn the crockery pot to HIGH. For every 2 cups of liquid in the crockery pot, dissolve 2 tablespoons of arrowroot or cornstarch in 2 tablespoons of cold water in a measuring cup. Stir the arrowroot or cornstarch mixture into the food in the slow cooker. Cook for about 5 minutes until the gravy is thick. Don't overstir or overheat. Arrowroot breaks down with too much stirring; cornstarch does with too much heat.

Flour: At the end of cooking, turn the crockery pot to HIGH. For every 2 cups of liquid in the crockery pot, dissolve 4 tablespoons of instant or regular flour in 4 tablespoons of cold water in a measuring cup. Stir the flour mixture into the food in the crockery pot. Cook about 5 minutes until thick.

Tapioca: At the start of cooking, stir tapioca into the ingredients in the crockery pot. Use 3 to 4 tablespoons of tapioca for every 2 cups of liquid.

Other Thickeners: Potato flakes as well as mashed potatoes, pureed rice, and pureed beans make excellent thickeners. To thicken with them, follow the directions given with individual recipes.

❧ CONVERTING FAMILY FAVORITES ❧

Do you have some favorite soups, stews, and main dishes that you'd like to adapt to crockery pot cooking? Converting recipes is remarkably easy, almost failure-proof, if you follow the guidelines presented here. Read "Cooking Basics" and "Secrets to Success" earlier in this chapter. Apply the techniques discussed there, and make the following adjustments as well.

Liquid: When converting a recipe for slow cooking, reduce the amount of liquid by at least half that required in the conventional recipe. Why? Very little liquid escapes during slow cooking. In fact, condensation forms on the lid, drips back onto the food, and keeps everything nicely moist. A single cup of water, juice, or broth is usually plenty. For soups, use just enough broth or water to cover the ingredients.

Time: When going from stove-top speedy to slow-cooker steady cooking, allow plenty of simmering time. You'll need to experiment with each recipe, but this is the general conversion: Quadruple the conventional cooking time to get the slow-cooker time on LOW. Double the conventional cooking time to get the slow-cooker time on HIGH.

STEWS

RATATOUILLE WITH FETA CHEESE

*Mediterranean style: This old-world favorite is full to the brim
with eggplant and fresh basil flavors. Few dishes
adapt better to unattended slow cooking.*

Large crockery pot

1 cup (240 ml) fat-free beef broth

1 cup (200 g) crushed tomatoes

1 can (16 ounces, 455 g) stewed tomatoes

2 medium onions, halved and sliced

1 medium zucchini, thinly sliced

½ pound (228 g) eggplant, peeled and cut into
 ½-inch (13 mm) cubes

4 cloves garlic, minced

1 yellow pepper, thinly sliced

1 teaspoon white wine vinegar

2 sprigs of lemon thyme

6 leaves fresh basil, snipped

2 ounces (56 g) feta cheese, crumbled

Combine the broth, tomatoes, and stewed tomatoes in the crockery pot. Stir in the onions, zucchini, eggplant, garlic, pepper, and vinegar. Add the lemon thyme. Cover and cook on LOW for 6 to 8 hours or on HIGH for 4 to 6 hours. Discard the lemon thyme and stir in the basil. Divide the stew among 4 bowls and sprinkle feta cheese over each serving.

Serves 4

- No lemon thyme available? Substitute a sprig of thyme and a strip of lemon peel.

Savory Kielbasa–Potato Stew

*This hearty pairing of Polish sausage and red potatoes is
low in calories, high in flavor, and will appeal to any appetite.
Green peas add a splash of bright color.*

Medium crockery pot

½ pound (228 g) cooked turkey kielbasa,
    thinly sliced

1 pound (455 g) red potatoes, diced

1 onion, cut into thin wedges

1 rib celery, sliced

2 cups (240 ml) water

2 packets low-sodium beef bouillon powder
    (or 2 teaspoons bouillon granules)

¼ teaspoon freshly ground
    black pepper

½ teaspoon dried savory

1 cup (150 g) frozen peas, thawed

Cook the kielbasa in a nonstick skillet over medium-high heat, stirring occasionally, until lightly browned, about 8 minutes.

Combine the kielbasa, potatoes, onions, celery, water, bouillon, pepper, and savory in the crockery pot. Cover and cook on LOW or HIGH until the vegetables are tender, 5 to 7 hours on LOW or 3 to 5 hours on HIGH.

Stir in the peas, and recover the pot. Cook the stew until the peas are crisp-tender, about 5 minutes.

Serves 4

- Two cups (480 ml) fat-free store-bought beef broth can replace the water and bouillon. Just be aware that the dish will have more sodium.

COUNTRY-STYLE CHICKEN STEW PROVENÇAL

Rustic stews like this one are loaded with sturdy vegetables and flavorful herbs. Enjoy carrots, potatoes, white beans, and mushrooms steeped in the special flavors of garlic and herbes de Provence.

Medium crockery pot

2 teaspoons olive oil

1 pound (455 g) boneless, skinless chicken breast, cut into 1-inch (2.5 cm) pieces

4 ounces (114 g) portobello mushrooms, cubed

1 can (14 ounces, 420 ml) fat-free chicken broth

¼ cup (60 ml) dry white wine

3 potatoes, sliced

1 can (15 ounces, 426 g) great northern beans, rinsed and drained

4 carrots, sliced

8 cloves garlic, minced

¼ teaspoon white pepper

1 teaspoon herbes de Provence

¼ cup (20 g) snipped fresh parsley, for garnish

Heat the oil in a large nonstick skillet over medium-high heat. Add the chicken and mushrooms, and sauté, stirring occasionally, until the chicken is lightly browned, about 8 minutes.

Combine the chicken mixture, broth, wine, potatoes, beans, carrots, garlic, and white pepper in the crockery pot. Cover and cook on LOW until the chicken is cooked through, the potatoes are tender, and the flavors are blended, 6 to 8 hours.

Season with the herbes de Provence and serve garnished with the parsley.

Serves 4

• Save time by simply scrubbing, and not peeling, the potatoes.

❧ RUSTIC CHICKEN STEW ❧

This chunky stew is easy to make and features chicken,
carrots, corn, and peas—all tastefully seasoned with thyme.

Large crockery pot

2 pounds (910 g) boneless, skinless chicken
breasts, cut into 1-inch (2.5 cm) cubes

3 medium onions, quartered

2 carrots, cut into 1-inch-thick (2.5 cm) slices

2 potatoes, cut into 1-inch (2.5 cm) cubes

2 cans (14 ounces, 420 ml) each),
fat-free chicken broth

1 teaspoon celery seed

1 teaspoon dried thyme leaves

½ teaspoon black pepper

8 ounces mushrooms, halved

1 cup (150 g) frozen corn

1 cup (150 g) frozen peas

Combine the chicken, onions, carrots, potatoes, and broth in the crockery pot. Stir in the celery seed, thyme, pepper, mushrooms, and corn. Cover and cook on LOW until the chicken is done and the vegetables are tender, 7 to 9 hours (or on HIGH 4 to 6 hours). Stir in the peas and cook until they're done, 15 to 30 minutes.

Serves 4

• Baby carrots make a quick and easy substitute for the
1-inch-thick carrot slices.

Turkey, Carrot, and Apple Stew

*At the end of a busy day, beat the clock with this sensational dish that
mixes sweet (apples and raisins) with spicy (curry and hot pepper sauce).*

Medium crockery pot

Olive-oil nonstick spray

1¼ pounds (568 g) boneless, skinless turkey
   breast slices, cut into strips

2 onions, cut into wedges

1 can (14 ounce, 420 ml) fat-free chicken broth

1 rib celery, sliced ¼ inch (6 mm) thick

½ cup (80 g) raisins

6 carrots, sliced ½ inch (13 mm) thick

1 teaspoon brown sugar

½ teaspoon curry powder

⅛ teaspoon ground turmeric

1½ cups (227 g) chopped McIntosh apples

2 tablespoons cornstarch

3 tablespoons cold water

1 teaspoon Louisiana hot sauce, or to taste

Coat a nonstick skillet with the spray and heat it over medium-high heat. Add the turkey and onions, and cook, stirring, until browned, 4 to 6 minutes.

Combine the turkey mixture, broth, celery, raisins, carrots, brown sugar, curry powder, and turmeric in the crockery pot. Cover and cook on LOW until the turkey is cooked through and tender, 6 to 8 hours.

Stir in the apples. Cover the crockery pot, and cook for 1 to 2 minutes to soften the apples.

In a small cup, whisk together the cold water and cornstarch. Stir into the turkey mixture, and cook until the sauce has thickened, 1 to 5 minutes.

Serves 4

- When McIntosh apples aren't in season, use almost any other popular apple: Cortland, Empire, Golden Delicious, Granny Smith, Rome Beauty, Winesap.

SOUPS

Hearty Corn Chowder with Peas

*Thick, flavorful chowders like this one are always a big hit
with my family. This potato–corn version gets a spicy kick from
Italian sausage and hot pepper sauce.*

2 teaspoons olive oil

2 ounces (57 g) Italian sausage, chopped
into ½-inch (13 mm) cubes

1 large onion, chopped

4 cloves garlic, minced

1 can (14 ounces, 420 ml) low-sodium
vegetable broth

2 russet potatoes, peeled and cut into
½-inch (13 mm) cubes

1 can (15 ounces, 426 g) cream-style corn

1 cup (150 g) frozen corn, thawed

½ cup (75 g) frozen peas, thawed

1 teaspoon Crystal brand Louisiana-style
hot sauce

Heat the oil in a skillet over medium-high heat. Add the sausage, onions, and garlic, and. sauté, stirring, until the sausage is lightly brown and the onions are translucent, 5 to 8 minutes.

Combine the sausage mixture, broth, and potatoes in the crockery pot. Cover and cook on LOW or HIGH until the potatoes are very tender, 5 to 6 hours on LOW or 3 to 4 hours on HIGH. Using the back of a spoon, coarsely mash the potatoes. Stir in the cream-style corn and the corn. Cover, turn the crockery pot to HIGH, and cook for 1 hour. Stir in the peas and cook until the mixture is hot and the peas are tender, about 10 minutes. Stir in the hot sauce.

Serves 4

- The intensity of hot sauces varies from mild, such as the Crystal brand used in this recipe, to scorching, such as Tabasco sauce. If using a variety other than Crystal, add it by the drop and taste-test after each addition.

❧ Fresh Manhattan Clam Chowder ❧

Never shucked a clam? No problem. Succulent minced clams are readily available in the fish section of most large supermarkets.

Large crockery pot

3 slices bacon

2 celery stalks, finely chopped

3 medium onions, finely chopped

4 small potatoes, diced

2 carrots, diced

½ teaspoon dried thyme leaves

¼ teaspoon black pepper

⅛ teaspoon Louisiana hot sauce, or to taste

1 pint minced clams or 2 cans (6½ ounces, 186 g, each)

1 can (28 ounces, 800 g) stewed tomatoes, cut up

½ cups (40 g) snipped fresh parsley

Cook the bacon in a skillet over medium-high heat until it's crisp, about 5 minutes. Drain the bacon on paper towels. Crumble the bacon into the crockery pot. Discard the drippings, leaving about 1 teaspoon in the skillet. Sauté the celery and onions in the bacon drippings in the same skillet until golden, 3 to 4 minutes. Transfer the onion mixture to the crockery pot. Stir in the potatoes, carrots, thyme, pepper, and hot sauce.

Drain the liquid from the clams into a pint measuring cup (480 ml). Add enough water to it to make 2 cups (480 ml) of liquid. Add the clam liquid–water mixture (not the clams) to the crockery pot. Stir in the tomatoes. Cover and cook on LOW for 6 to 8 hours or on HIGH for 4 to 6 hours. During the last hour of cooking, stir in the minced clams. Cover and cook for 1 hour. Stir in the parsley and cook for 15 minutes.

Serves 8

- Fresh minced clams shouldn't smell fishy. If they do, return them to the store for a truly fresh batch. This chowder will keep for up to 3 days in the refrigerator.

❧ RED BEAN AND SALAMI SOUP ❧

Just a little salami provides unique flavor in this simple soup.
I've used red kidney beans, but pinto or a combination of kidney
and pinto beans would be just as tasty. If your family and friends
are anything like mine, they'll request this basic soup often.
But don't tell them how easy it is to toss together.

Medium crockery pot

2 teaspoons olive oil

1 small onion, chopped

6 cloves garlic, minced

1 small white eggplant, chopped

**2 cans (14 ounces, 420 ml, each)
fat-free beef broth**

1 can (15 ounces, 426 g) diced tomatoes

**1 can (15 ounces, 426 g) red kidney beans,
rinsed and drained**

1 small zucchini, sliced

2 ounces (57 g) hard salami, chopped

½ teaspoon freshly ground black pepper

4 sprigs thyme

Heat the oil in a large nonstick skillet over medium-high heat. Add the onions, garlic, and eggplant. Sauté, stirring frequently, until the eggplant is lightly browned, about 10 minutes. Add ¼ cup of the broth and stir to deglaze the skillet.

Combine the eggplant mixture, remaining broth, tomatoes with juice, beans, zucchini, salami, pepper, and thyme in the crockery pot. Cover and cook on LOW or HIGH until the vegetables are tender and the flavors are blended, 5 to 6 hours on LOW or 3 to 4 hours on HIGH. Discard the thyme sprigs.

Serves 6

- If thyme sprigs are young and tender, mince and add them to the soup. If they're woody oldsters, use them whole and discard them after cooking.

❧ VEGETABLE SOUP FOR ALL SEASONS ❧

*Fall, winter, and summer vegetables star in this mostly vegetable soup.
Can't find white turnips? Then substitute rutabagas, also known as
swedes or Swedish turnips. To make a vegetarian version,
replace the chicken broth with vegetable broth.*

Large crockery pot

1 teaspoon olive oil

2 leeks, white part only, thinly sliced

6 cloves garlic, minced

3 cans (14 ounces, 420 ml, each)
    fat-free chicken broth

3 white potatoes, peeled and chopped

2 white turnips, peeled and shredded

1 small yellow squash, cubed

1 carrot, shredded

2 bay leaves

¼ teaspoon white pepper

1 small green bell pepper, chopped, for garnish

Heat the oil in a nonstick skillet over medium-high heat. Add the leeks and garlic, and sauté, stirring, until lightly browned.

Combine the leek mixture, broth, potatoes, turnips, squash, carrots, bay leaves, and white pepper in the crockery pot. Cover and cook on LOW until the potatoes are tender, 5 to 6 hours. Discard the bay leaves.

Divide among 8 bowls. Garnish each serving with the bell peppers.

Serves 8

- Leeks can be a sandy lot. To clean them, cut off the root ends and trim the tops. Split lengthwise and swish in lots of cold water.

CREAM OF TOMATO SOUP

Move over canned soup . . . this freshly made one rates tasters' choice. Its preparation is almost as simple as the store-bought version—honest.

Medium crockery pot

1 can (28 ounces, 855 g) plum tomatoes, cut up

1 can (14 ounces) fat-free beef broth

1 medium onion, finely chopped

1 teaspoon butter

1 teaspoon Louisiana hot sauce

½ teaspoon dried thyme leaves

1 teaspoon sugar

½ cup (100 g) rice

2 teaspoons red wine vinegar

¼ teaspoon black pepper

½ cup (120 ml) half-and-half (or light cream)

Combine the tomatoes, broth, onions, butter, hot sauce, thyme, sugar, rice, vinegar, and pepper in the crockery pot. Cover and cook on HIGH for 3½ to 5 hours. Using a hand-held blender, puree the soup. Stir in the half-and-half.

Serves 4

• Fresh out of half-and-half? Substitute canned evaporated skim milk; the taste and texture will be just fine.

HAM AND BLACK BEAN SOUP WITH CHILIES

Shredded carrots add a splash of color to this peppery soup.

Medium crockery pot

Nonstick spray

½ pound (228 g) lean ham, finely chopped

2 cans (14 ounces, 420 ml, each) fat-free beef broth

1 can (15 ounces, 426 g) black beans, rinsed and drained

Coat a skillet with nonstick spray and warm it over medium-high heat. Brown the ham, about 5 minutes. Transfer it to the crockery pot.

Stir in the broth, beans, onions, chilies, sweet peppers, carrots, bay leaf, and cumin. Cover and cook on LOW for 6 to 8 hours or on HIGH for 4 to 6 hours. Discard the bay leaf.

Serves 6

2 medium onions, chopped

2 medium-hot chili peppers (such as jalapeño, serrano, or poblano), finely chopped

1 large sweet green pepper, chopped

2 carrots, coarsely shredded

1 bay leaf

½ teaspoon cumin seeds

- If you prefer a less nippy soup, use only 1 medium-hot chili or substitute a mild variety, such as Anaheim.

❧ SWEET SAUSAGE AND WHITE BEAN SOUP ❧

*So simple. So tasty. So easy to make that you can
whip up this rustic soup for a fuss-free weeknight dinner.
Serve with a crusty bread for sopping up the flavorful broth.*

Medium crockery pot

2 ounces (57 g) cooked sweet Italian sausage, thinly sliced

1 can (14½ ounces, 414 g) stewed sliced tomatoes

1 can (14½ ounces, 540 ml) fat-free beef broth

2 cups (450 g) rinsed and drained canned cannellini beans

1 large carrot, thinly sliced

1 potato, finely chopped

3 sprigs thyme

1 tablespoon chili sauce

Combine the sausage, tomatoes, broth, beans, carrots, potatoes, thyme, and chili sauce in the crockery pot. Cover and cook on LOW or HIGH until the carrot and potato are tender, 5 to 6 hours on LOW or 3 to 4 hours on HIGH. Discard the thyme sprigs.

Serves 4

 Onion-Leek Soup

For a healthful indulgence in French onion soup,
be sure to try this slow-simmered version with a Swiss twist.

Large crockery pot

2 leeks, white part only, thinly sliced

3 medium onions, thinly sliced and
  separated into rings

1 teaspoon olive oil

4 cloves garlic, pressed

1 cup (240 ml) vegetable broth

3 cups (720 ml) water

1½ tablespoons white wine vinegar

2 bay leaves

4 fresh sage leaves

⅛ teaspoon white pepper

¼ cup (20 g) shredded reduced-fat
  Swiss cheese

2 cups garlic croutons

Sauté the leeks and onions in the oil in a nonstick skillet over medium-high heat until lightly browned. Transfer the vegetables to the crockery pot. Stir in the garlic, broth, water, vinegar, bay leaves, sage, and white pepper. Cover and cook on LOW for 6 to 8 hours or on HIGH for 4 to 6 hours. Discard the bay leaves. Divide the soup among 4 bowls, and top each serving with a quarter of the cheese and croutons.

Serves 4

• To make 2 cups garlic croutons, cut approximately 4 slices of firm bread into fl-inch cubes. Place the cubes on a baking sheet or a perforated pizza pan. Mist the cubes with nonstick spray, and sprinkle them with garlic powder. Broil them until they're golden, about 5 minutes. Shake or stir the cubes to expose the uncooked sides; broil them until golden, about 3 minutes.

Meatball and Bow Tie Pasta Soup

Tiny meatballs made with cheese and basil
fill this hearty soup with irresistible flavor.

Medium crockery pot

½ pound (228 g) ground round beef

½ cup (40 g) quick-cooking oats

2 tablespoons dried minced onions

2 teaspoons garlic powder

2 teaspoons dried basil

1 egg white

½ cup (44 g) grated Parmesan cheese

1 can (15 ounces, 426 g) whole tomatoes, cut up

3 cups (720 ml) fat-free beef broth

1 cup (180 g) baby carrots, halved lengthwise

1 zucchini, halved lengthwise and sliced ½ inch (13 mm) thick

4 ounces (114 g) bow tie pasta (farfelle)

Combine the beef, oats, 1 teaspoon of the onions, ½ teaspoon of the garlic, ½ teaspoon of the basil, egg white, and ¼ cup (22 g) of the cheese in a bowl. Shape the mixture into sixteen 1-inch-diameter meatballs. Heat a nonstick skillet over medium-high heat. Add the meatballs and cook until brown, about 8 minutes.

Combine the remaining onions, the remaining garlic, the remaining basil, the tomatoes, broth, carrots, zucchini, and meatballs in the crockery pot. Cover and cook on LOW until the meatballs are cooked through and no longer pink and the flavors are blended, 5 to 6 hours.

Cook the pasta according to package directions. Drain well and stir into the meatball-vegetable mixture. Divide among 4 bowls and top each serving with the remaining ¼ cup (22 g) cheese

Serves 4

● Be sure to form firm meatballs; loosely shaped ones may fall apart during cooking.

VEGETABLES & SIDES

❧ Herbed Potatoes and Carrots ❧

*The natural sweetness of carrots pairs perfectly with
the tart flavor of lemmon. This easy recipe uses the herb lmon thyme.*

Medium crockery pot

2 carrots, cut into ½-inch (13 mm) slices

2 medium potatoes, cut into ½-inch
(13 mm) cubes

4 large scallions, white part only, cut into
½-inch (13 mm) slices

¼ cup (60 ml) vegetable broth

Dash of freshly ground black pepper

Sprig of lemon thyme or ¼ teaspoon dried
thyme leaves

The natural sweetness of carrots pairs perfectly with the tart flavor of lemon. This easy recipe uses the herb lemon thyme.

Place the carrots, potatoes, and scallions in the crockery pot. Add the broth, pepper, and thyme. Cover and cook on HIGH until the vegetables are tender, 4 to 6 hours. Discard the lemon thyme.

Serves 4

❧ Pierogies in Pepper-Shallot Sauce ❧

*Here a chunky, robust sauce enhances
the less intense flavors of potato-filled pierogies.*

Large crockery pot

1 can (28 ounces, 800 g) crushed tomatoes

1 shallot, thinly sliced

1 cup (171 g) chopped sweet green peppers

½ teaspoon olive oil

½ tablespoon red wine vinegar

½ teaspoon Italian herb seasoning

½ teaspoon black pepper

1 pound (455 g) potato-filled pierogies,
fresh or frozen

Combine the tomatoes, shallots, peppers, oil, vinegar, seasoning, and black pepper in the crockery pot. Cover and cook on LOW for 5 to 9 hours or on HIGH for 3½ to 5 hours. Add the pierogies. Cover and cook for 1 hour.

Serves 6

• Pierogies are Polish filled dumplings. Thaw frozen pierogies before adding them to the sauce.

❧ Black Bean and Corn Chili ❧

Create a stir with knockout chili that's full of beans and other healthful vegetables.

Medium crockery pot

1 can (14–19 ounces, 400-540 g) black beans, rinsed and drained

1 can (28 ounces, 800 g) tomatoes, cut up

1 large green bell pepper, chopped

2 large onions, chopped

1½ cups (211 g) corn

1 chili pepper, seeded and chopped

4 cloves garlic, minced

2 tablespoons chili powder

2 teaspoons ground cumin

1 teaspoon dried oregano

Combine the beans, tomatoes, bell pepper, onions, corn, chili pepper, garlic, chili powder, cumin and oregano in the crockery pot. Cover and cook on LOW or HIGH until the flavors are blended, 5 to 6 hours on LOW or 3 to 4 hours on HIGH.

Serves 4

❧ New-Fashioned Baked Beans ❧

This incredibly easy and great-tasting recipe makes enough for a small crowd. Why not simmer up a potful for your next potluck supper?

Medium crockery pot

3 cups (600 g) crushed tomatoes

2 cans (15 ounces, 426 g, each) great northern beans

½ pound (228 g) Canadian bacon, cut into ¼-inch (6 mm) cubes

1 medium onion, minced

¼ cup brown sugar

1 tablespoon coarse brown mustard

2 tablespoons red wine vinegar

½ teaspoon hickory smoke flavoring

Combine the tomatoes, beans, bacon, onions, sugar, mustard, vinegar, and smoke flavoring in the crockery pot. Cover and cook on LOW for 7 to 9 hours.

Serves 10

• These spicy-sweet beans keep in the refrigerator for 3 to 4 days. Small white beans or white kidney beans can be substituted for the great northerns.

❧ CREAMY TURNIPS WITH CHEESE ❧

Delight family, friends, even finicky eaters
with this smooth dish of potatoes, turnips, and two cheeses.

Medium crockery pot

1¼ cups (300 ml) fat-free chicken broth

1 pound (445 g) turnips, peeled and cut into ½-inch (13 mm) pieces

1 pound (445 g) potatoes, peeled and cut into ½-inch (13 mm) pieces

½ cup (121 g) nonfat ricotta cheese

¼ (28 g) cup shredded sharp cheddar cheese

¼ teaspoon white pepper

Paprika, garnish

Combine the broth, turnips, and potatoes in the crockery pot. Cover and cook on LOW or HIGH until the vegetables are very tender, 5 to 6 hours on LOW or 3 to 4 hours on HIGH.

Using a potato masher, a hand-held immersion blender, or a hand-held mixer, mash the turnip–potato mixture, blending in the ricotta cheese, cheddar, and white pepper. Garnish each serving with the paprika and serve.

Serves 4

- The peak season for turnips is October through February. For tender, sweet-tasting turnips, get young ones—they'll be small and heavy for their size. Oldsters tend to be large and woody and have a strong flavor.

❧ MAPLE-CANDIED SWEET POTATOES ❧

Raisins and maple syrup bring out the natural sweetness
of these golden potatoes. Serve them often; they're a snap to fix.

Medium crockery pot

¼ cup (87 g) maple syrup

¼ cup (60 ml) apple juice

1 tablespoon butter

4 small sweet potatoes, peeled

½ cup (80 g) raisins

Mix the syrup and juice in the crockery pot. Add the butter, potatoes, and raisins. Cover and cook on LOW until the potatoes are tender, 8 to 10 hours. Serve with the syrup from the crockery pot and raisins spooned over the potatoes.

Serves 4

❧ ROSEMARY'S SAUCY GREEN BEANS ❧

*Believe it or not, these beans are crisp-tender even after simmering for hours.
And their flavor? It's the greatest!*

Medium crockery pot

1 pound (445 g) fresh green beans

1 can (28 ounces, 800 g) crushed tomatoes

2 strips crisp bacon, crumbled

4 cloves garlic, minced

1 teaspoon dried rosemary

⅛ teaspoon freshly ground
    black pepper

Combine the beans, tomatoes, bacon, garlic, rosemary, and pepper in the crockery pot. Cover and cook on LOW until the beans are tender, 5 to 7 hours.

Serves 8

● Though their flavor's not as intense, 2 tablespoons of store-bought bacon-flavored bits or 2 slices of minced Canadian bacon can replace the crumbled bacon.

❧ CURRIED BUTTERNUT SQUASH ❧
WITH CILANTRO

*The distinctive and intriguing flavor of curry dominates in this fast-to-fix
side dish. Serve with roast chicken or turkey.*

Medium crockery pot

¼ cup (60 ml) fat-free chicken broth

2 medium butternut squash, peeled and cut into
    1-inch (2.5 cm) cubes

1 tablespoon curry powder

⅛ teaspoon freshly ground black pepper

4 sprigs of fresh cilantro, snipped

Pour the broth into the crockery pot. Toss the squash with the curry, and add it to the crockery pot. Cover and cook on LOW until the squash is tender, 6 to 8 hours. Transfer to a serving bowl and sprinkle with the pepper and cilantro.

Serves 8

● After 6 to 8 hours of cooking, the squash is very tender. For firmer squash, cook 4 to 5 hours.

GARLIC MASHED POTATOES

Garlicky spuds like these are a hot item in many trendy restaurants.
Fortunately, duplicating the flavor is satisfyingly simple.

Medium crockery pot

6 potatoes, peeled and quartered

8 cloves garlic, minced

1 tablespoon minced dried onions

2 cups (480 ml) water

Pinch of white pepper

¾ cups (180 ml) milk

Combine potatoes, garlic, onions, and water in the crockery pot. Cover and cook on LOW or HIGH until the potatoes are very tender, 5 to 6 hours on LOW or 3 to 4 hours on HIGH.

Drain and remove the potatoes to a bowl. Using a potato masher, mash the potatoes with pepper and milk; finish by whipping them with an electric mixer, if desired.

Serves 4

- Too rushed to peel and chop eight cloves of garlic? Use 4 teaspoons minced garlic from a jar instead.

SAVORY TURNIP BOWLS WITH BACON AND ONIONS

Here's a clever turnip presentation that's company-special yet everyday easy.

Medium rectangular crockery pot

½ cup (120 ml) low-sodium vegetable broth

2 large white turnips, (12 ounces, 341 g, each), scrubbed

1 medium potato, quartered

Pour the broth into the crockery pot. Slice a thin piece from the bottom of each turnip so the turnips sit flat. Using a melon baller, scoop out the interior of each turnip, leaving a ¼-inch

1 small onion, quartered

1 tablespoon snipped fresh dill or
    1 teaspoon dried dillweed

2 slices crisp bacon, crumbled

⅛ teaspoon freshly ground black pepper

(6 mm) shell and reserving the interior. Place the shells in the crockery pot.

Shred the reserved turnip, potatoes, and onions in a food processor. Mix in the dill and bacon. Spoon the turnip mixture into the shells. Cover and cook on LOW until the turnip is tender, 3 to 5 hours. Sprinkle with the pepper.

Serves 2

- To cook 4 or more turnip bowls at once, use an electric skillet. Set the heat to simmer.

TOMATOES STUFFED
WITH BEANS AND RICE

*In this recipe, juicy ripe tomatoes serve as bowls
for a satisfying, creamy filling of refried beans and rice.
The flavors — cumin, chili, and peppers — are superbly Southwestern.*

Medium crockery pot

4 large tomatoes

½ cup (100 g) cooked long-grain rice,
    such as Basmati

1 small onion, chopped

½ green bell pepper, chopped

½ cup (114 g) fat-free refried beans

¼ cup (20 g) chopped fresh parsley

¼ teaspoon cumin seeds

½ teaspoon chili powder

½ teaspoon crushed red pepper flakes

¼ cup (60 ml) salsa with cheese

Slice the tops off the tomatoes. Using a melon baller, scoop out the pulp and place it in a sieve. Using the back of a wooden spoon, press out the juice, discarding it, and chop the tomato pulp.

Combine 1 cup (200 g) of pulp (set the remaining pulp aside for another use), rice, onions, peppers, refried beans, parsley, cumin seeds, chili powder, and pepper flakes in a bowl. Spoon into the tomatoes.

Pour 2 tablespoons of water into the bottom of the crockery pot. Arrange the tomatoes, in 2 layers if necessary, in the crockery pot. Cover and cook on LOW until hot and flavorful, 3 to 4 hours.

Serves 4

- Leave the sides of the tomatoes about ¼- to ½-inch (7-13 mm) thick when removing the pulp; thick sides will help the tomatoes retain their shape during cooking.

POULTRY

❧ Orange–Basil Chicken ❧ with Fruit Salsa

For sensational, refreshing flavor, you can't beat this fruit-and-poultry entrée.
If perfect pears aren't available, substitute a red- or green-skinned apple in
the salsa. This recipe will charm its way onto your menu often, guaranteed.

Medium crockery pot

1 chicken breast (about 3 pounds, 1.4 kg)

1 orange, thinly sliced

12 fresh basil leaves

1 cup (240 ml) fat-free chicken broth

1 orange, sectioned and diced

1 pear, diced

1 shallot, thinly sliced

1 teaspoon olive oil

1 tablespoon cider vinegar

Dash of ground red pepper

1 teaspoon dry sherry

Lift the chicken's skin and slide the orange slices and 10 basil leaves under it. Coat a large nonstick skillet with cooking spray and heat over high heat. Add the chicken and cook until nicely browned, turning occasionally, 10 to 12 minutes. Place in the crockery pot. Pour ½ cup (120 ml) of the broth into the same skillet and cook, stirring and scraping, for 2 minutes to deglaze the skillet. Pour into the crockery pot and add the remaining ½ cup (120 ml) broth. Cover and cook on LOW until the chicken is cooked throughout, its juices run clear, and a meat thermometer registers 170° F, 7 to 9 hours.

Meanwhile, mince the remaining 2 basil leaves. In a small bowl, combine the diced orange, pear, shallot, oil, vinegar, red pepper, sherry, and minced basil. Cover and refrigerate until ready to serve.

Divide the chicken into thirds. Freeze two-thirds for later use. Slice the remaining chicken, discarding the skin, oranges, and basil. Serve immediately with the orange-pear mixture.

Serves 4

- The technique of sliding seasonings under poultry skin also works well for whole chickens, turkeys, and Cornish hens.

American Paella

Wild rice makes classic Spanish paella an American main course. Complete this delicious one-dish meal with a favorite dessert.

Large crockery pot

2⅓ cups (560 ml) fat-free chicken broth

1½ large red onions, coarsely chopped

3 cloves garlic, finely chopped

½ pound (228 g) boneless, skinless chicken
    breasts, cut into 1-inch (2.5 cm) cubes

1 jar (4 ounces (114 g) roasted peppers, drained

1 teaspoon turmeric

½ teaspoon dried thyme leaves

⅛ teaspoon black pepper

⅓ cup (65 g) wild rice

1 cup (200 g) long-grain brown rice

½ pound (228 g) shrimp, shelled
    and deveined

1 cup (150 g) frozen peas

Combine the broth, onions, garlic, chicken, roasted peppers, turmeric, thyme, and black pepper in the crockery pot. Cover and cook on HIGH for 3 to 5 hours.

Stir in the shrimp and wild and brown rices. Cover and cook until the shrimp and rices are tender and most of the liquid has been absorbed, about 1¼ to 2 hours. Add more water while the rice is cooking, if needed. Stir in the peas and cook until they're tender, about 15 minutes.

Serves 6

47

 CHICKEN STROGANOV

Named after Count Paul Stroganov, a 19th-century Russian diplomat, traditional stroganov is rich with butter, beef, and sour cream. This twenty-first-century version packs the same intriguing flavors but has far less fat.

Medium crockery pot

1 pound (455 g) boneless, skinless chicken breasts, cut into 1-inch (2.5 cm) cubes

4 teaspoons olive oil

2 medium onions, chopped

1½ cups (115 g) mushrooms, sliced

½ cup (120 ml) dry white wine

¼ teaspoon black pepper

1 teaspoon paprika

½ cup (120 g) nonfat sour cream

8 ounces (228 g) broad egg noodles

Paprika, for garnish

In a skillet over medium-high heat, brown the chicken on all sides in 2 teaspoons of the oil, about 5 minutes. Transfer the chicken to the crockery pot.

In the same skillet over medium-high heat, sauté the onions and mushrooms in the remaining oil until the onions are golden, 3 to 4 minutes. Transfer the onion mixture to the crockery pot. Pour in the wine, and sprinkle the onion mixture with the pepper and paprika. Cover and cook on LOW until the chicken is tender and cooked through, 7 to 9 hours. In the last half-hour of cooking, cook and drain the noodles separately; keep them warm.

Using a slotted spoon, transfer the chicken to a platter, leaving the onion mixture and liquid in the crockery pot. Keep the chicken warm. Stir the sour cream into the onion mixture. Serve the chicken over the hot noodles, top with the sour cream sauce, and garnish with the paprika.

Serves 4

SAVORY TURKEY MEATBALLS IN ITALIAN SAUCE

These meatballs have the taste of those grandmom used to make, but only a fraction of the fat. Enjoy them with spaghetti or in a hoagie roll.

Medium crockery pot

1 can (28 ounces, 800 g) crushed tomatoes

1 tablespoon red wine vinegar

1 medium onion, finely chopped

2 cloves garlic, minced

Combine the tomatoes, vinegar, onions, garlic, seasoning, and basil in the crockery pot. Cover and turn crockery pot on to LOW. In a bowl, mix the turkey, egg whites, garlic powder, dried onions, pepper, oats, parsley, and cheese. Form into 16 one-inch balls, and dredge each ball in the flour. Lightly mist the balls with the non-

¼ teaspoon Italian herb seasoning

1 teaspoon dried basil

1 pound (455 g) ground turkey breast

2 egg whites

⅛ teaspoon garlic powder

¼ teaspoon dried minced onion

⅛ teaspoon black pepper

$^1/_3$ cup (27 g) quick oats

$^1/_3$ cup (27 g) dried parsley

¼ cup (21 g) grated Parmesan cheese

¼ cup (35 g) unbleached flour

Nonstick spray

stick spray and brown them on all sides in a nonstick skillet over medium-high heat. Transfer them to the crockery pot. Cover and cook on LOW for 8 to 10 hours.

Serves 8

• These keep nicely in the freezer for up to a month.

❧ CREAMY CHICKEN ❧
WITH ROASTED PEPPERS

Here's an updated fast and flavorful version of chicken à la king. If you like, you can stir in ½ cup (74 g) fresh or frozen peas shortly before cooking is done.

Medium crockery pot

2 teaspoons olive oil

¾ pound (340 g) chicken, cut into
    ¾-inch (20 mm) pieces

1 onion, chopped

2 ribs celery, thinly sliced

4 ounces (113 g) portobello mushrooms,
    chopped

¾ cup (80 g) chopped roasted red peppers

1 can (10 ounces, 300 ml) reduced-fat
    cream of celery soup

¼ cup (60 ml) dry white wine

¾ cup (180 ml) fat-free milk

4 English muffins, split and toasted, or "bake
    and fill" puff pastry shells

Heat the oil in a large skillet over medium-high heat. Add the chicken, onions, celery, and mushrooms. Cook, stirring occasionally, just until the chicken is lightly browned, about 10 minutes.

Combine the chicken mixture, red peppers, soup (undiluted), and wine in the crockery pot. Cover and cook on LOW until the chicken is cooked through and the flavors are blended, 6 to 8 hours. Stir in the milk and cook until heated through, 10 to 15 minutes.

Serve immediately over the muffins or in the shells.

Serves 4

• Portobello mushrooms are firmer and meatier than white button mushrooms, but if you can't find the portobello variety, select and slice the button variety. Use store-bought roasted red peppers in a jar to save time.

❧ CHICKEN PARMESAN ❧

In this simple dish, the classic duo of tomatoes and cheese takes
chicken from ordinary to extraordinary. Mark the recipe for future reference.
It's so tasty, you'll have numerous requests to serve it often.

Medium crockery pot

2 teaspoons olive oil

4 skinless, boneless chicken breasts (about
    3 ounces, 85 g, each)

1¼ cups (250 g) crushed tomatoes

2 large cloves garlic, crushed

1 teaspoon sugar

Pinch of celery seeds

2 tablespoons dry red wine

½ cup (55 g) shredded mozzarella cheese

2 tablespoons grated Parmesan cheese

Heat the oil in a nonstick skillet over medium-high heat. Add the chicken and sauté, stirring occasionally, until lightly browned, about 10 minutes.

Combine the chicken, tomatoes, garlic, sugar, celery seeds, and wine in the crockery pot. Cover and cook on LOW until the chicken is cooked through and a meat thermomter registers 170° F, 6 to 8 hours.

Combine the cheeses in a small bowl and sprinkle them over the chicken. Don't stir. Cook until the cheeses are melted, about 15 minutes.

Serves 4

• To save time, select store-bought shredded and grated cheeses; but to get maximum flavor, freshly shred and grate the cheeses.

CHINESE CHICKEN WITH VEGETABLES

Subtly seasoned with five-spice powder,
this recipe captures the essence of a Shanghai-style dish.

Medium crockery pot

2 strips bacon

1 pound (455 g) boneless, skinless chicken
    breast, cut into 1-inch (2.5 cm) pieces

1 cup thinly sliced celery

1 medium potato, cut into ½-inch
    (13 mm) cubes

1 cup sliced scallions

1 can (8 ounces, 228 g) bamboo shoots

1½ teaspoons five-spice powder

½ cup (120 ml) water

1 tablespoon dry sherry

1 tablespoon low-sodium soy sauce

2 tablespoons cornstarch

1 teaspoon sugar

Cook the bacon in a skillet over medium heat until crumbly, about 5 minutes. Drain on paper towels, crumble, and transfer to the crockery pot.

Pour off all but 2 teaspoons of the bacon drippings, and add the chicken to the skillet. Brown the chicken on all sides; then transfer it to the crockery pot. Stir in the celery, potatoes, scallions, bamboo shoots, five-spice powder, ½ cup (120 ml) of the water, and the sherry and soy sauce. Cover and cook on LOW until the chicken is cooked through and tender, 6 to 8 hours. In a measuring cup, combine the cornstarch, remaining water, and sugar. Pour into the chicken mixture and cook until the liquid has thickened, about 3 minutes.

Serves 4

- Five-spice powder, a pungent blend of cinnamon, cloves, fennel seed, star anise, and Szechuan peppercorns, is available in Asian markets and in most supermarkets. For added color, garnish with thin strips of sweet red pepper.

MEATS

HERITAGE PORK ROAST

A braised roast with mustard-sage seasoning and a side of
apple-flavored sweet potatoes. Serve with a light spinach salad.

Large crockery pot

½ cup (120 ml) apple juice or cider

1½ pounds (680 g) sweet potatoes, peeled
    and sliced 1 inch (2.5 cm) thick

3 medium onions, sliced and separated
    into rings

4 medium apples, peeled and sliced

2 pound (910 g) center-cut boneless
    pork roast, trimmed of fat

1 teaspoon Dijon mustard

¼ teaspoon black pepper

4 fresh sage leaves, snipped, or
    ⅛ teaspoon dried sage

¼ cup (60 ml) cold water

1 teaspoon brown sugar

2 tablespoons cornstarch

Pour the apple juice into a crockery pot. Then layer the sweet potatoes, onions, and apples in the crockery pot.

In a nonstick skillet, brown the pork on all sides over medium-high heat. Place the pork on top of the potato and apple slices. Brush the mustard over the roast and sprinkle the roast with the pepper and sage. Cover and cook on LOW until the roast is done and registers 165°F (73.9°C) on a quick reading meat thermometer, 7 to 9 hours.

Transfer the roast to a platter and keep it warm. Using a slotted spoon, transfer the apple–sweet potato mixture to a bowl and keep it warm.

Combine the water, sugar, and cornstarch in a measuring cup. Stir the cornstarch mixture into the juices in the crockery pot, and cook, stirring often, until they thicken, 1 to 2 minutes. Serve it over the apple-potato mixture and the roast.

Serves 6

- Don't be surprised if the apples seem to disappear during cooking; their wonderful, sweet flavor remains.

German-Style Sauerbraten

Traditional sauerbraten simmers for hours on the stove top.
This oven version has been simplified, and features the same
great flavors found in classic recipes.

Medium crockery pot

1 cup (240 ml) fat-free beef broth

1 large onion, cut into thin wedges

2 cloves garlic, minced

1 teaspoon mixed peppercorns (sometimes called pepper melange)

1 tablespoon pickling spice

1 bay leaf

2 cups (480 ml) dry red wine

1 teaspoon coriander seeds

1 pound (455 g) beef rump roast, trimmed of fat

½ cup (about 12 cookies) gingersnap crumbs

½ cup (120 g) fat-free sour cream

In a glass bowl, combine the broth, onions, garlic, peppercorns, pickling spice, bay leaf, wine, and coriander. Add the beef. Cover and marinate in the refrigerator for 24 hours, turning once or twice.

Remove the beef and marinade to the crockery pot. Cover and cook on LOW until the beef is very tender and a meat thermometer registers at least 160°F or 71°C, 8 to 10 hours.

Remove the beef to a platter, reserving the broth mixture, and cover to keep warm. Pour the broth mixture through a strainer into a 2-quart (liter) saucepan. Discard the spices and onions. Stir the gingersnaps into the broth. Cook, stirring, over medium heat until thickened. Stir in the sour cream.

Slice the meat and serve topped with the broth mixture.

Serves 4

• Whole peppercorns, whole allspice, and whole mustard seeds can be substituted for the mixed peppercorns and pickling spice.

Sagely Seasoned Pork Sirloin Roast

Wonderfully subdued and slightly minty, sage plays a dual role in
this recipe: It boostes flavor and keeps the roast moist at the same time.
If you can't find fresh sage, try basil leaves or sprigs of rosemary.

Large crockery pot

2¼ (540 ml) cups fat-free beef broth

¼ cup (60 ml) dry white wine

1 onion, chopped

Combine broth, wine, onion, pepper, celery, and garlic in the crockery pot. Add the pork. Press the mustard seeds into the pork above the liquid. Arrange the sage over the mustard. Cover and cook on LOW until the pork is cooked through and a meat ther-

½ red bell pepper, chopped

1 rib celery, chopped

1 clove garlic, minced

3-pound (1.4 kg) pork sirloin roast, trimmed of fat

2 teaspoons yellow mustard seeds

8 to 10 fresh sage leaves

1 cup (200 g) wild pecan rice

1 tablespoon pine nuts, toasted

mometer registers 160°F or 71°C, 8 to 10 hours. Let rest for 10 minutes before slicing and serving.

Meanwhile, cook the rice according to package directions. Add the nuts and toss to combine.

Divide the roast into thirds. Freeze two-thirds for later use. Slice the remaining roast and serve with the rice.

Serves 6

- Look for pine nuts under these names: pine nuts, Indian nuts, piñon nuts, pignoli, and pignolia.

MUSTARD-CRUSTED POT ROAST WITH POTATOES

Here's an updated pot roast with easy preparation and exceptional flavor.
Mustard seeds and crushed peppercorns form a pleasing piquant crust;
slow-cooking creates a tender roast. This recipe is top notch. Take my word for it!

Medium crockery pot

2¼ (540 ml) cups fat-free beef broth

2½-pound (1.1 kg) eye of round roast, trimmed of fat

¼ cup (60 ml) dry red wine

1 small onion, quartered

1 rib celery, quartered

1 small carrot, quartered

1 clove garlic, minced

1 bay leaf

1 teaspoon freshly ground black pepper

2 teaspoons black or yellow mustard seeds

6 potatoes, halved

Combine the broth, beef, wine, onion, celery, carrot, garlic, and bay leaf in a crockery pot. Press the pepper and mustard seeds into the beef above the liquid. Arrange the potatoes around the beef. Cover and cook on LOW until the beef is very tender and a meat thermometer registers at least 160°F or 71°C, 8 to 10 hours.

Remove the beef and potatoes to a serving platter, reserving the liquid. Discard the onion, carrot, celery and bay leaf. Slice the beef and serve with the potatoes and reserved cooking liquid.

Serves 8

- Don't worry if the roast rests atop chunks of onion and carrot while it cooks. Press the pepper and mustard firmly into the meat.

BASIL MEATBALLS IN TOMATO SAUCE

Generous amounts of basil brighten the flavor of these
traditional beef favorites. Serve over spaghetti or in rolls.
The hearty meatballs be an instant hit.

Medium crockery pot

¾ pound (340 g) ground sirloin

½ cup (40 ml) quick oats

1 teaspoon dried oregano

¼ cup (15 ml) chopped fresh basil leaves

1 egg white

¼ cup (20 g) grated Romano cheese

¼ cup (35 g) unbleached flour

2 tablespoons olive oil

1 can (28 ounces, 800 g) crushed tomatoes

1 onion, chopped

4 cloves garlic, minced

¼ cup (60 ml) dry red wine

Combine the beef, oats, Italian seasoning, basil, egg white, and cheese in a large bowl. Form into 1-inch (2.5 cm) balls and dredge in the flour.

Heat the oil in a large nonstick skillet over medium-high heat. Add the meatballs and cook, turning frequently, until browned, about 10 minutes.

Combine the tomatoes, onion, garlic, wine and meatballs in the crockery pot. Cover and cook on LOW or HIGH until the meatballs are cooked through and the flavors are blended, 5 to 6 hours on LOW or 3 to 4 hours on HIGH.

Serves 4

• Form very firm meatballs and let them cook for several minutes before turning. That way, they won't fall apart.

• These meatballs freeze quite nicely for up to a month. So why not double the recipe and freeze half for another day?

MUSHROOM-STUFFED BEEF ROLL-UPS

Here I use a store-bought stuffing to minimize prep time and maximize flavor. It's a handy ingredient for those times when speed is essential.

Medium crockery pot

4 thin beef round steaks (about 3 ounces, 85 g each)

Olive-oil cooking spray

4 ounces (114 g) mushrooms, chopped

1 onion, chopped

1 rib celery, chopped

1 cup seasoned stuffing mix

2 cups (480 ml) fat-free beef broth

1 tablespoon dry red wine

1 bay leaf

3 tablespoons cold water

2 tablespoons cornstarch

Freshly ground black pepper, garnish

Using a meat mallet, pound the steaks to ¼ inch (6 mm) thick.

Coat a nonstick skillet with the cooking spray and heat over medium-high heat. Add the mushrooms, onions, and celery, and sauté, stirring, until the mushrooms and onions are lightly browned.

In a bowl, combine the mushroom mixture, stuffing mix, and ½ cup (120 ml) of the broth. Place a spoonful of the stuffing mixture in the center of each steak; roll up and fasten with a toothpick.

Heat the nonstick skillet again; add the roll-ups and cook until they're browned on all sides. Transfer to the crockery pot. Pour in the wine and the remaining ½ cup (120 ml) broth. Add the bay leaf. Cover and cook on LOW until the beef is cooked through and very tender, 6 to 8 hours.

Remove to a platter, reserving the broth; keep the beef warm. Discard the bay leaf. Pour the broth into a saucepan.

Combine the cornstarch and cold water in a measuring cup. Pour into the broth and cook, stirring, over medium heat until thickened, about 2 minutes. Serve the roll-ups with the thickened broth. Sprinkle the pepper over each serving.

Serves 4

- Chop the mushrooms, onions, and celery fairly fine. Small pieces make it easier to roll up the stuffing and beef.

❦ ROAST LEG OF LAMB PROVENÇAL ❦

*A sophisticated entrée, this tender leg of lamb begs for inclusion
in company-special dinners. Present it with mashed garlic potatoes
or a rice pilaf and a green vegetable such as broccoli, asparagus, or peas.*

Large crockery pot

3 pounds (1.4 kg) lamb shank

1 teaspoon olive oil

1 teaspoon herbes de Provence

4 cloves garlic, sliced

1 cup (240 ml) fat-free beef broth

1 tablespoon dry red wine

Coat a large nonstick skillet with cooking spray and heat over high heat. Add the lamb and cook, turning often, until brown on all sides, 5 to 10 minutes. Let cool slightly.

Combine the oil and herbes de Provence in a small bowl. Cut small slits in the lamb with a sharp paring knife. Stuff with the garlic slices. Rub the herbes de Provence mixture over the lamb.

Pour the broth and wine into the crockery pot. Add the lamb. Cover and cook on LOW until the lamb is cooked through and a meat thermometer registers at least 160°F or 71°C, 8 to 10 hours. Let rest for 10 minutes before slicing and serving.

Serves 8

❦ BEER-BRAISED POT ROAST ❦

*Not your run-of-the-mill pot roast: this one sports a piquant, full-bodied
gravy that's seasoned with garlic, bay leaf, cinnamon, and turmeric.*

Medium crockery pot

Cooking spray

2 pounds (910 g) top round beef roast, trimmed of visible fat

6 onions, quartered

6 cloves garlic, pressed

8 ounces (228 g) mushrooms, quartered

12 ounces (360 ml) beer or nonalcoholic beer

1 bay leaf

Coat a nonstick skillet with the cooking spray, and heat over medium-high heat. Add the beef, and cook, stirring occasionally, until brown, 5 to 10 minutes. Remove to the crockery pot and add the onions, garlic, mushrooms, beer, and bay leaf. Cover and cook on LOW until the beef is very tender and a meat thermometer registers at least 160°F or 71°C, 8 to 10 hours.

Remove the beef to a platter, reserving the beer-onion mixture; keep the beef warm. Discard the bay leaf. Pour the beer-onion mixture into a saucepan.

½ cup (120 ml) cold water

¼ teaspoon ground turmeric

Pinch of ground cinnamon

2 teaspoons browning and seasoning sauce

¼ cup (35 g) flour

16 ounces (455 g) wide noodles

In a small measuring cup, combine the water, turmeric, cinnamon, browning sauce, and flour. Pour into the beer–onion mixture and cook, stirring, over medium heat until thickened.

Meanwhile, cook the noodles according to package directions. Drain well.

Slice the beef, and serve with the beer–onion mixture and noodles.

❧❧❧ BEEF ROAST WITH ❦❦❦
MUSHROOM-ONION GRAVY

Pot roast never tasted so good or was so easy to prepare.

Large crockery pot

3 pounds (1.4 kg) bottom-round beef, trimmed of fat

3 medium onions, finely chopped

8 ounces (228 g) mushrooms, thickly sliced

Butter-flavored nonstick spray

½ cup (120 ml) dry red wine

¼ teaspoon black pepper

¼ cup (60 ml) cold water

2 tablespoons cornstarch

1 teaspoon browning sauce

Brown the roast on all sides in a nonstick skillet over medium-high heat, 5 to 6 minutes; transfer to a crockery pot. In the skillet, sauté the onions until golden, about 3 minutes; transfer them to the crockery pot. Add the mushrooms to the same skillet, lightly coat with spray; sauté until golden, about 3 minutes. Transfer the mushrooms to the crockery pot.

Pour the wine into the crockery pot; sprinkle the roast with the pepper. Cover and cook on LOW until the roast is tender, 8 to 10 hours. Transfer the roast to a platter, leaving the onions, the mushrooms and liquid in the crockery pot. Keep the roast warm.

Combine the cold water, cornstarch and browning sauce in a measuring cup. Stir the cornstarch mixture into the onion-mushroom gravy, and cook, stirring often, until the gravy thickens, 2 to 3 minutes. Slice the roast; serve topped with gravy.

Serves 12

• The meat freezes well for up to a month. The gravy, once thickened with cornstarch, won't freeze well, but it'll keep in the refrigerator for a day or two.

SAVORY LAMB CHOPS

An unusual threesome of mint, chilies, and rosemary jazzes up these lamb chops. The rich, spicy sauce that accompanies the chops is ideal for giving a sprightly twist to potatoes or noodles as well.

Medium crockery pot

1 can (14 ounces, 420 ml) fat-free
    beef broth

4 sprigs fresh mint

¾ pound (340 g) lamb shoulder chops,
    trimmed of fat

2 ounces (57 g) fresh chives, chopped

2 poblano chilies, seeded and chopped

¼ teaspoon freshly ground black pepper

1 tablespoon fresh rosemary leaves

¼ cup (36 g) precooked cornmeal (such as
    Masarepa®) or instant flour

1 teaspoon browning and seasoning sauce

Combine the broth, mint, lamb, chives, chilies, black pepper, and rosemary in the crockery pot. Cover and cook on LOW or HIGH until the lamb is tender, 5 to 6 hours on LOW or 3 to 4 hours on HIGH.

Remove the lamb to a platter, reserving the cooking liquid, and cover with foil to keep warm. Skim fat from the reserved liquid. Stir in the cornmeal and browning sauce, and cook, stirring, until thickened. Serve over the chops.

Serves 4

- Precooked cornmeal and instant flour dissolve quickly and lump free in hot liquids.

❧ JAMAICAN JERK PORK ❧

*This trendy entrée gets its flavorful, hot zing from a rub with eight spices,
including pungent cloves and nippy peppers.*

Medium crockery pot

2 cups (480 ml) fat-free beef broth

2 teaspoons dried minced onions

1 teaspoon dried thyme

1 teaspoon garlic powder

1 teaspoon crushed red pepper flakes

¼ teaspoon ground cinnamon

¼ teaspoon powdered ginger

¼ teaspoon allspice

pinch of ground cloves

1 pound (455 g) pork tenderloin

3 tablespoons cold water

2 tablespoons cornstarch

Pour the broth into the crockery pot.

In a small bowl, combine the onions, thyme, garlic, red pepper flakes, cinnamon, ginger, allspice and cloves. Rub the spice mixture into all sides of the pork. Place the pork in the crockery pot.

Cover and cook on LOW until the pork is cooked through and a meat thermometer registers 160°F or 71°C, 6 to 8 hours. Let rest for 10 minutes before slicing and serving.

Remove to a platter, reserving the broth; keep the pork warm. Pour the broth into a saucepan.

In a small cup whisk together the cold water and cornstarch. Stir into the broth, and cook, stirring, over medium heat until slightly thickened. Slice the pork and serve topped with the thickened broth.

Serves 4

- Some supermarkets carry jerk seasoning. If yours does, give the prepared combo a try.

CORNED BEEF WITH RED CABBAGE

Corned beef and cabbage, cooked in a crockery pot? Absolutely.
The meat is deliciously tender and the flavors are superb. Oh, and
you don't need to wait until St. Patrick's day to serve this delightful dinner.

Medium crockery pot

1½ pound (680 g) corned eye of round beef, trimmed of fat

6½ cups (1.5 l) water

4 bay leaves

9 peppercorns

¼ cup (60 ml) red wine vinegar

6 russet potatoes

6 cups coarsely sliced red cabbage

Combine the beef, water, bay leaves, peppercorns, and vinegar in the crockery pot. Arrange the potatoes around the beef. Cover and cook on LOW until the beef is very tender and a meat thermometer registers at least 160°F or 71°C, 8 to 10 hours.

Add the cabbage, cover, and cook until tender, about 15 minutes. Discard the bay leaves.

Serves 6

- So the cabbage pieces stay together during cooking, leave a bit of core with each slice or wedge.

❧ Red- and Black-Bean Chili ❧

Perfect for fall and winter suppers, this spicy dish packs plenty of healthful fiber. Serve with carrot and celery crudités and crusty sourdough bread.

Large crockery pot

1 pound (455 g) extra lean ground beef

6 cloves garlic, minced

3 large onions, chopped

2 large sweet green peppers, chopped

2 chili peppers, minced

1 can (28 ounces, 800 g) crushed tomatoes

1 cup (240 ml) water

4 cups home-cooked red kidney beans, or 2 cans
    (15 ounces, 426 g, each), rinsed and
    drained

2 cups home-cooked black beans, or
    1 can (16 ounces, 455 g), rinsed
    and drained

3 tablespoons chili powder

1 teaspoon ground cumin

¼ teaspoon ground allspice

¼ teaspoon ground coriander

1 tablespoon red wine vinegar or
    cider vinegar

Brown the beef in a nonstick skillet over medium-high heat, until the meat is browned and crumbly, about 3 minutes. Spoon off the fat as it accumulates. Add the garlic and onions, and cook until the onions are translucent, about 3 minutes.

Transfer the beef mixture to a crockery pot. Add the sweet peppers and chili peppers, tomatoes, water, red and black beans, chili powder, cumin, allspice, coriander, and vinegar. Cover and cook on LOW for 6 to 8 hours.

Serves 8

• This hearty chili tastes superb the second day. Store it in the refrigerator, and reheat it until hot and bubbly.

PORK CHOPS NIAGARA

A New York state wine, with its characteristic subtle
Concord grape flavor, makes this a deliciously different entrée.
For a complete meal, accompany the dish with a light salad.

Medium crockery pot

4 boneless center-cut loin pork chops, sliced ½ inch (13 mm) thick and trimmed of fat (about 1 pound, 455 g)

1 teaspoon olive oil

4 cloves garlic, crushed

½ teaspoon white pepper

1½ cups (360 ml) white wine (for example, New York State Niagara Grape)

2 shallots, thinly sliced

1 tomato, sliced

½ green bell pepper, thinly sliced in rings

4 potatoes, quartered

Rub the pork with the oil, garlic, and pepper.

Coat a nonstick skillet with cooking spray and heat over medium-high heat. Add the pork and cook until lightly browned on both sides, about 3 minutes a side. Remove to a crockery pot.

Pour half the wine into the skillet, and cook, stirring and scraping to deglaze the skillet, about 3 minutes. Pour into the crockery pot. Arrange the shallots, tomatoes, and bell peppers over the pork. Arrange the potatoes around the edges of the crockery pot. Pour in the remaining wine. Cover and cook on LOW or HIGH until the pork is cooked through, the potatoes are tender, and the flavors are blended, 5 to 6 hours on LOW or 3 to 4 hours on HIGH.

Serve the pork topped with the broth and vegetables.

Serves 4

- To deglaze the skillet, bring the wine to simmering and stir, loosening bits of browned food.

DESSERTS

Heavenly Poached Pears

*Topped with luscious almond cream, these spicy pears make a
grand finale worthy of the fanciest dinner party, but are easy to make.*

Large crockery pot

Juice of 1 lemon

1 cup (240 ml) water

8 slightly underripe Bartlett, Anjou, or Bosc
   pears, peeled

2 tablespoons crystallized ginger

2 teaspoons lemon peel

2 tablespoons white sugar

5 tablespoons brown sugar

1 teaspoon ground cinnamon

2 cups (480 ml) white grape juice

for the Almond Cream:

1 cup (240 g) plain low-fat yogurt

1 cup (240 g) nonfat sour cream

½ teaspoon almond extract

Place the lemon juice and water in a medium bowl; dip the pears into the lemon mixture to keep them from browning. Stand the pears up in a crockery pot.

Combine the ginger, 1 teaspoon of lemon peel, white sugar, 2 tablespoons of brown sugar, cinnamon, and grape juice in a measuring cup; pour the juice mixture over the pears. Cover and cook on LOW until the pears are tender, about 5 hours. Remove the pears from the heat and let them cool in the poaching liquid.

To Make the Almond Cream: While the pears are cooking, drain the yogurt in a cheesecloth-lined strainer in the refrigerator. When ready to serve the pears, combine the drained yogurt (yogurt cheese), sour cream, remaining brown sugar, and almond extract; stir until well blended. Serve each pear with a dollop of almond cream; garnish with the remaining peel.

Serves 8

Mocha Bread Pudding

Hooked on chocolaty-coffee flavors? Then you'll adore this pudding.
It's satisfyingly rich-tasting and, like most bread puddings,
is best when made with a hearty country-style bread.

Medium crockery pot

4 tablespoons cocoa

1 cup (240 ml) hot coffee

1 egg

¼ cup (60 ml) fat-free egg substitute

2 cups (480 ml) low-fat (1%) milk

1 cup (240 ml) fat-free milk

½ cup (100 g) sugar

1 teaspoon vanilla

6 slices dry firm white bread, cubed

½ teaspoon ground cinnamon

Nonfat whipped topping (optional)

Whisk the cocoa into the coffee in a small bowl or a 2-cup (480 ml) measure. Let cool.

While the coffee is cooling, lightly beat the egg and egg substitute in a large bowl. Stir in the coffee mixture, low-fat milk, fat-free milk, sugar, vanilla, and bread. Pour into the crockery pot. Sprinkle with the cinnamon.

Cover and cook on LOW until a knife inserted into the center of the pudding comes out clean, 2½ to 3½ hours. Serve warm, at room temperature or chilled. And top with the whipped topping if using.

Serves 6

• Store in a covered container in the refrigerator for up to 3 days.

PEACH AND APPLE COMPOTE

*An after-dinner winner, this compote, which has nary a gram of fat,
will surely satisfy your sweet tooth. It's great for breakfast and snacks, too.*

Medium crockery pot

1 cup (92 g) dried peach halves

1 cup (56 g) dried apple slices

½ cup (80 g) golden raisins

½ cup (85 g) currants

1 cup (228 g) dried apricot halves

1 cinnamon stick

2½ cups (600 ml) water

Juice of 1 lemon

1 teaspoon grated lemon peel

1 tablespoon brown sugar

Frozen nonfat vanilla ice cream or yogurt
   (optional)

Combine the peaches, apples, raisins, currants, apricots, and cinnamon in the crockery pot. Stir in the water, lemon juice and peel, and sugar. Cover and cook on LOW until the fruit is tender, 5 to 7 hours. Discard the cinnamon stick. Serve with ice cream or yogurt, if you wish.

Serves 8

• Stir the cooked fruit gently. The compote keeps, covered, in the refrigerator for several days.

WALNUT-RAISIN-APPLE BAKE

*Looking for a carefree, applicious dessert? This sweet treat
will fill the bill. Serve it with your favorite nonfat frozen topping.*

Large rectangular crockery pot

½ cup (120 ml) apple cider

Juice of 1 lemon

2 teaspoons maple syrup

2 tablespoons raisins

1 tablespoon dark brown sugar

Pour the cider, lemon juice, and maple syrup into the crockery pot.

Combine the raisins, sugar, cinnamon, and walnuts in a small bowl. Place the apples in the crockery pot. Using a spoon, fill the center of the apples with the raisin mixture. Cover and cook on LOW until the apples are tender, 2 to 3 hours.

Serves 4

1 teaspoon ground cinnamon

1 teaspoon ground walnuts

4 large Macintosh apples, cored

- Like firm baked apples? Replace the Macintosh apples with Golden Delicious.

❧ PUMPKIN PUDDING ❧

An old-fashioned custardy pudding that'll evoke fond memories of holiday desserts. The best part: It's nutritious and delicious.

1 egg

2 egg whites

1½ cup (680 g) canned or home-cooked pureed pumpkin

2 cans (12 ounces, 360 ml, each) evaporated skim milk

1 teaspoon light margarine

⅓ cup (160 g) brown sugar

⅓ cup (67 g) white sugar

1 teaspoon ground cinnamon

½ teaspoon ground allspice

½ teaspoon ground nutmeg

½ cup raisins or chopped dates

2 cups packed soft bread cubes

1½ (360 g) cups brandied yogurt topping

For Brandied Yogurt Topping:

2 cups (485 g) low-fat vanilla yogurt

Cheesecloth

1 teaspoon brandy extract

Medium crockery pot

Beat the egg and egg whites together until they're a light lemon color. Combine the eggs, pumpkin, milk, and margarine in the crockery pot. Stir in the sugars, cinnamon, allspice, nutmeg, raisins or dates, and bread cubes. Cover and cook on LOW until a knife inserted in the center of the pudding comes out clean, 5½ to 7½ hours.

Serves 8

- Cook's note: To make brandied yogurt topping, place 2 cups (485 g) low-fat vanilla yogurt in a cheesecloth-lined strainer or colander. Let it drain in the refrigerator while the pudding is cooking. Stir 1 teaspoon brandy extract into the drained yogurt.

❧ POACHED PEARS WITH RASPBERRY GLAZE ❧

Here, I offer a 3-D dessert:
delightfully easy, delightfully attractive, delightfully delicious.

Medium crockery pot

6 cups (1.4 l) cran-raspberry
    juice cocktail

2 cups (480 ml) unsweetened
    apple juice

1 cinnamon stick

2 lemon or orange tea bags

4 firm Bosc or Anjou pears, peeled

¼ cup (60 ml) raspberry preserves, melted

Combine the juices, cinnamon, tea bags, and pears in the crockery pot. Cover and cook on LOW or HIGH just until the pears are tender, 3 to 4 hours on LOW or 1½ to 3 hours on HIGH.

Discard the cinnamon stick and tea bags. Let the pears cool in the mulled juice. Using a slotted spoon, remove the pears to dessert plates, reserving the mulled juice for another time, and drizzle the pears with preserves. Serve immediately.

Serves 4

• The reserved cinnamon-raspberry poaching juice from this recipe makes for a singular sweet-tart mulled beverage. To serve it as a mid-afternoon pick-me-up, simply warm the juice on the stove top or in the crockery pot. Serve it in mugs, and use additional cinnamon sticks as stirrers.

• Top the pears with a dollop of vanilla low-fat yogurt.

INDEX